On Blank Pages

On Blank Pages

Giuliano Enciso

For Mom.

My life is dedicated to you.
This page is just to tell you "I love you."

I.   The Part Of Your Past That Arrived
          Too Early

Pen To Paper

I've missed you old friend.

It's been awhile, I thought we might have lost each other. But no matter how long it's been, this feels comfortable, catching up with you always feels right. This feels like home.

And it's good to be back.

<u>Hobbes</u>

On days when I've stopped believing in myself, you treat me like an imaginary friend. You're the only one that still sees me. I'm glad we haven't quite grown up yet.

Insert Coin To Play

Dear player 2, don't be afraid to jump into my game.
This extra quarter's for you.

Contrails

They will look at you and marvel at the heights you've reached, but they will underestimate the time they have to appreciate you. You will be gone before they know it, chasing the sun and leaving smoke trails for us to remember you by.

<u>Captions</u>

I miss your voice.

But it's not like I can just open an old photo album and remember what it sounds like. Instead, I'll listen for you in the notes you've written on the backs of photographs, hearing you speak through your handwriting.

Cornerstone

You are a rock, stable and strong. You carry every
expectation, every burden, and every weight on your
shoulders as the foundation of this family. And
while the years may have worn you down, and
weathered you, you remain standing. I only remind
you that if you need help, do not be afraid to ask for
it. I will do what I can to share your load. I promise
you're world won't collapse if you let me help you.
But my world will, if I lose you.

<u>Say Cheese</u>

There was a time when I used to smile in family pictures. There was a time where being happy didn't feel like a special occasion I'd visit once in a while. A time where my smile wasn't something I was told I had to wear. When family meant more than just the people I only see during the holidays. I don't remember the exact moment the family was removed from the pictures, but I think that was when I stopped smiling.

<u>Hallways</u>

Churches and hospitals.
These are two places in which I have never felt
comfortable since you left. Because when you came
here looking to find a savior, looking for answers,
searching for hope, for life, I lost everything.
Instead, what I found were reminders of death.

In The Dark

To be honest, I don't know the exact reason why I talk to myself. Maybe it's the fact that hearing a voice, even if it's your own, makes this house feel less empty. Because growing up feeling alone, the faces of no one were the only ones I felt comfortable telling secrets to, the walls were the only ones that ever listened to what I had to say, and the silence was the only voice that ever spoke to me without judgement.

Secondhand

She gave it up. Cold turkey. She knew that it would take a toll on her, on her body, and her mind. But she stopped. She quit for me as soon as she found out I'd be born, with no hesitation. But you, you've never quit, it was never worth the time or effort. 10 years later, she was gone. Today, you still smoke that garbage, inhaling and exhaling, spreading your poison cloud.

I was her first priority, but I'll always just be secondhand to you.

25

He gave me a quarter to use, in case I ever needed to call him. It's funny how times change, how things lose their value, how people drift and relationships fade, how life happens. I left the coin on top of a payphone. Maybe someone else could use it.

Kite Strings

She let me fly as high as I wanted to, watching from a distance. If there was any danger of an impending storm or threatening tree lines, she'd reel me in just enough. She never wanted to ground me, just keep me out of harm's way. It was her guidance that taught me how to fly. From time to time, I find myself caught in the rain, or stuck in branches that I can't get myself out of. I wish you could just pull me in again, I wish I still had you to come back to.

Bargaining

I don't believe in you.

I mean, I haven't for a while now. But I need you to be real, to somehow exist. Let's face it, I'm not going to walk up your staircase. I'm not getting in through those pearly gates, I'm a pretty terrible person. I'm fine watching from a distance, but I just need you to be real right now so I know that she's somewhere.

That she's okay.

That she's happy.

Because she deserves to have all that.

She deserves better.

16

Visits

Visiting your parents. It's kind of a weird thing to get used to, with the first few times maybe happening when you're in college, or maybe soon after. It's a stepping stone that usually means you've found independence. You've become an adult, sort of.

When you visit your parents, it means a lot of things, but mostly reminders of how real adults live. Cleaned laundry, fresh bed sheets, and home cooked meals. Actual meals. And not pizza. For breakfast. Again. Visiting your parents is a reminder of what you've missed most. It's love so warm, like it came right out of the dryer. Visiting your parents is kisses and hugs at the door. It's frequently hearing "how's school?" sometimes "are you taking care of yourself?" but it's always "I'll see you soon." Visiting your parents means coming home.

Visiting your parents is kind of a weird thing. I still miss her cooking. I still miss her hugs so warm that I was convinced they came out of the dryer. I miss her kisses at the door. I miss her helping with school. I miss her making sure I took care of myself.

Visiting your parents is kind of a weird thing, which I never got used to.

Because the thing about visiting your parent, the thing about visiting your mom, is it's not supposed to be visiting her at hospitals, not when you're 12. It's not supposed to be having to see her on a schedule. It's not supposed to involve chemotherapy or morphine. It's not supposed to be hugs and kisses goodbye bedside, instead of the doorway. It's not supposed to be leaving her, not this way. It's not supposed to be this hard. It's supposed to be I'll see you soon.

It's supposed to be I'll see you soon.

Waiting Rooms

Quiet hallways of hospitals hold some of the loudest pains I can vaguely remember. I don't remember much though, except waiting.

There was a television set. There's always a television set. Probably to help you forget. I still remember the color of her eyes that day, they weren't hazel or brown anymore. I remember the fact that she couldn't speak, but they said she loved me.

This was my least favorite memory. Waiting. Waiting in hallways and not in her room. I don't know why I chose to stay out in these hallways, but that's exactly where I sat. Waiting. Waiting to lose my mother.

Capes

It no longer mattered who wore the pants in this family. My mother wore the cape. And you can keep your gender stereotypes, because my mother was Superman. She wasn't bulletproof but made you believe she was because she never cried. Not in front of us. Maybe she did, behind closed doors, where she'd always put on that cape, so we wouldn't see her be anything but heroic. But the only real difference between her and Superman was that he crumbled at the sight of kryptonite. And she, well, she was diagnosed with it. There was no running from it, no hiding from it. Unlike comics, she fought her battles from morning to night, with no alter ego to hide behind. She couldn't imprison her villains, but forced to face them constantly, and fight the kinds of battles that don't take place in comic books.

Unlike Superman, I can't just write a new version and resurrect the hero back unto these pages. I can't unwrite your death. I can't be the one to fly back around the world and bring you back to life. I can't save you. Because I'm not the one that's wearing the cape.

& Telephone Booths

The greatest strength I've ever come to witness was something I had very little understanding of at the time. It's the strength found in dying. The strength and resolve to keep it all together when everything is falling apart around you. To be patient in the face of unanswered questions, to carry faith after unanswered prayers. The greatest strength I've ever witnessed was the ability of a person to live in the face of death, as if no such thing existed. The greatest strength I've had the chance to be a part of was the day my mother chose to shave her head, give us the clippers, and prove heroes are still super without their capes, letting us know she was still mom without her hair.

She Knows Best

"I wish you could have met her."

> It's what I'll tell my mom about you.
> It's what I'll tell you about her.

"You would have liked her."

II.   The Part Where You Fall In Love

<u>Unsaid</u>

You'll never know the first time I told you I loved
you. It was late at night and you fell asleep after one
of our longer conversations. The type of
conversations that have you fighting fatigue.
I don't remember what we were talking about,
but I remember knowing how I felt about you.
The first time I told you I loved you,
you couldn't say it back, but it still felt right.
The first time I told you I loved you,
it was practice for the rest of my life.

<u>Hi</u>

"Hi"

These two letters sent from your mouth to my ears
don't need stamps. They ignore long distances,
surpass weather conditions, and are never late. Not
always expected but always loved and appreciated.
They are envelopes with my name sprawled across
the backs in your handwriting, sealed with your lips,
wanting to be opened, with notes of conversations
waiting to be read. And I'll always return to sender
with two letters of my own.

"Hi"

Big Bang Theory

I want to be so unequivocally lost at night in our conversation that I can't even see a way out until the light of the old sun on a new day finds cracks between the clouds. All I need is you, to focus on for the next few hours; "tired" holds no definition, and "time" actually ceases to exist. Really. In fact, your voice alters time, and changes my reality. It's hard to remember what things were like before you came around. Boom! Explosions of light and sound create this incomprehensible moment in my mind. I've come to understand why it's taking so long to put my universe back together. It happens every time I think of you.

Tidal

Like the way ripples turn into tsunamis, our small
talks have a tendency to form my biggest memories.

Umbrella

Share an umbrella with me. I'll protect you from the storm.

And tomorrow, I'll feed you chicken noodle soup. Because you'll get sick. Because you didn't want to share that umbrella with me. Instead, you said, "I want to dance in the rain, because no one dances in the rain." And so we danced.

And jumped in puddles; and got our socks wet. And closed our eyes, listening to the sounds of the rain. And when it came down even harder, I kissed you.

And tomorrow, I'll feed you chicken noodle soup.

But right now, I'll ask you to share this umbrella with me, because the rain can't stop me from falling in love with you today.

Stockholm Syndrome

You hold my thoughts hostage throughout the day, and I don't have the heart to let go. I can't escape you. You stole my heart and make me want to break every rule in the book, I want to be your partner in crime. Trapped in your arms, locked in your embrace, and throw away the key. I'll do the time if I can spend the next 25 to life with you.

Vacation

Let's take a vacation and just get away together. You can take me on a tour of your thoughts. I want to spend a day wandering around your mind. You can take me to your favorite spots, we can visit your best memories. And if we find ourselves in alleys of dark secrets, I'll do my best to let you know you're safe with me.

Girl With The Red Lipstick

I imagine that feeling your wine glass knows when your lips leave it, is the same one as your smile gives my heart. My memory still holds the stains you left on my mind.

Forecast

There's a 15% chance of showers, but a 100% chance I'll fall in love with you. I can't predict the weather, but I'll always take the odds when it comes to us.

Second Edition

Let's pretend for a second that we never met, so we can fall in love all over again, and rewrite our story. Maybe if we take a step back and revise the mistakes, we'll get the ending we hoped to find.

Cloud Chasers

I loved the girl chasing sunsets as much as I loved the girl who ran from the moonlight. There wasn't much I could do then, except chase sunsets with her, and when it escaped us, to just be there to hold her hand until the sun disappeared. I hoped she knew I'd still be there staring at the sky even when there was no more light.

Message in a Bottle

I sat here, with the sun falling behind the horizon.
The water was calm, but the waves inside clashed
from the storms that lay within. My feet dug deep in
the sand. My hands skimmed atop the grains. I
could smell the ocean air. The day began to fade but
I held its beautiful simplicity in my mind and heart. I
filled an old wine bottle, cleaned out, with just a
handful of sand. The way the grains fell was
reminiscent of those hourglass or sand timers I've
seen in old antique shops. I hesitated, wondering if
there was enough sand, but eventually sealed the
glass neck with a cork. As the night came, the stars
followed. The day had reached its exodus. My time
had run out here. And so, with a hopeful naivety, I
found myself knee deep in the water as I set the
bottle down. Maybe this little piece of the world
where I am will reach you wherever you are.

All-Nighter

Can we have one more night where our
conversations carry us on clouds straight through
until morning? Where there's no need for caffeine,
or energy drinks, we'll just sip on each other's words,
getting drunk on each other's voice. Where I forget
what tired feels like. And when I ask you if you're
tired yet, I'm hoping you say no. Where if my eyes
close, I can still hear your voice. When if my eyes
close, you'll still be there when I open them again. I
think maybe, I've had too much sleep lately. I could
use a sleepless night with you.

<u>Breath Mints</u>

Our talks are refreshing.

24 Hours

I will keep my neon light shining with doors open for you. Let me be your comfort food, your late night craving, your somewhere to go when everywhere else is closed.

White Paint

I will draw pictures of you on the walls of this room, and then paint over them in coats of white, only to retrace our history again, and again. I imagine I've drawn the outline of your smile a million times over, or at least somewhere close to it. My walls have started to cave in with these thoughts of you.

Caffeine

You are the addiction that keeps me up all night.
You are the only one I want to wake up to.

Two Roads

Love is choosing the person you care about over the dreams you've chased. Real love is never asking someone to make that choice.

Your heart knows best, follow it. Even if that direction is away from me.

Galoshes

I've never had cold feet when it came to us.
We'll run through the rain, and let it drown out the
impending doubt. I am ready to take leaps of faith
into puddles with you.

Shoestrings

Grab my hand, and let our fingers intertwine like laces on a pair of shoes. I know we still have that fresh out-of-box type of love, but whenever you let go, and you untie yourself from me, I start to come undone, and find myself tripping over my own thoughts. Come back, stay with me, and I promise I'll double knot our laces so our heartstrings never come apart again.

The Storm

You are the torrential downpour approaching
without notice. I am nowhere close to being
prepared for you, standing in the middle of nowhere
with no shelter in sight. You come without warning,
without hesitation and without mercy.

Existentialism Of The Storm

Why has it always been easiest to write about rain? Why are storms so romantic and intriguing? What is it about danger that draws us in? I ask these questions, but know too well the answers. Because it is on the brink of death where we feel most alive. That opposing force that allows us to realize the presence of the other. I cannot live without knowing death, the same way I cannot love without feeling heartbreak, or immense joy without crippling depression. I speak about the rain because I'm chasing the sunsets I won't feel the need to write about.

Ante Meridiem

She waits on the doorstep of every dream, tapping
slowly at my subconscious, reminding me to come
home to her in the morning as she greets me with
slow kisses to open my door.

<u>Tectonics</u>

She hardly speaks, but when she does, she makes the very ground I stand upon tremble. I can feel the vibrations of the way she whispers my name. She drifts into my thoughts, shifting into my mind throughout the day.

I remember nothing before we collided. The only world I know is the one she's shaped.

<u>Rogue</u>

I will love you.
I will love you,
even when you no longer understand why.
When you've refused to stay,
long after you've gone.
Against all logic and reason.
Because of my rebel heart,
I will still love you.

Finders Keepers

You weren't looking for me, but here I was, turning
up unexpectedly.
You'll whisper,
"Can I keep you?"

And I'll answer,
"Finders keepers"

Long Distance

This is where "good morning" meets "goodnight".

Where "I love you's" come packaged in shoeboxes.
They come in pairs, and are no good without each
other.
Where dates through webcams become reasons to
cancel plans. Because they're the only plans.
Where letters are more than just part of an alphabet,
but part of our history.
This is where "goodbyes" are not meant for forever,
but ongoing promises to return.
Where love is tested. Where most love dies.
But where only the strongest loves survive.

So tell me "goodnight" this morning and I'll wish
you "sweet dreams" with my coffee.

III.   The Part Where You Fall Apart

Coffee Break

We sat there, the sun glistening, beautiful and radiant. The day was promising and full of potential. She greeted me with a "Good morning" as she sat, delicately, across from me sipping my coffee.
I turned to catch her smile, soft and warm, like the sun hitting my face, and was hit by a beam of reality. I no longer found solace in her eyes, no comfort in her words, no warmth in her touch.
No truth, no honesty, no hope.
And that was it. No hope. We were no longer a "we". No substance. Just empty.
I stared at my cup. A coffee ring stain. Faded. Much faded after the washings but permanent after so long.
Rising from my downward stare, I looked at her with dismay. She gazed back at me, perplexed.
"Do you want more?"
"No..."
"...I think I'm done."

Addiction

Hi.

Hi.

Hi…

Hi?

Hi Pretty Girl.

Relapse.

The Sound Of Nostalgia

I miss your voice. It echoes through my head like music bouncing off the walls of an empty hall. I can't remember the lyrics, but your voice still plays my favorite song. Your kiss still lingers on the cusp of my lips, I can almost taste it on the tip of my tongue. If I keep humming your melody, maybe you'll come back to me. If I stop, the only thing I'll hear is the sound of silence.

Lost

I do a really bad job of keeping things. I have this awful tendency to forget and lose things. Like keys. Or my phone. Or love. Typically, it doesn't take too long to find what you're looking for, but with love, it's a bit more difficult. It's tough because they say "don't look for love, let it find you"; but it's hard when all I want to do is put up lost posters, and offer a reward to the person that brings you back. I hope one day you look down, and engraved on your heart is the address that leads you home to me.

Crazy

The jacket I wear is eggshell white, and has buckles and straps on it. The four walls of my bedroom are covered in padding, and I spend hours staring at my ceiling because there are no windows. I have no music to listen to so I'm forced to listen to the voices in my head, with the loudest one being the one that sounds like you. The girl of my dreams has transformed into the ghost that haunts my nightmares. My arms are restrained because the doctors are scared I'll hurt myself. Because I'm still picking up the pieces of my shattered heart to slit my wrists, hoping to feel something again.

The Love Thief

Steal my heart like a thief in the night. Captivate me throughout the day, invade my mind when it gets dark. Shoot me glances that take my breath away. And I am left empty when you go.

<u>Imprint</u>

You came into my life without warning, and left without a trace. But not really, because I still see pieces of you everywhere I go. Your fingerprints are everywhere, including all over my heart. I see you everywhere, in shadows on the wall, footprints in the ripples from puddles in rain storms, in illusions that plague my dreams. What hurts isn't that you've forgotten me, it's that I can't forget you.

Plagiarized

I walked out of the patent office with them laughing at me, thinking I was crazy. I tried to copyright my emotions. I wanted to protect my heart after she stole it. I don't think she'll ever credit me for loving her.

Hide And Seek

I was anxious to find you but excited to play. It took some time, but when I found you, I was happy. It feels different now though, to be the one sitting in the dark. I'm hoping we're still playing the same game, that you're still looking, that you haven't forgotten about me.

<u>Bridges</u>

I'm sorry I let this bridge burn. I know I let our
memories turn into ashes.
But then I remembered how you always enjoyed
playing with matches.

You stand across this river with nothing connecting
us, nothing left to say.
I hear the smell of gasoline is hard to wash away.

<u>Daisy</u>

She pulled away from me like petals from a flower, letting the wind take her from my hands. In hindsight, she always kissed me with daisy lips, some days she loved me, and other days she loved me not. Still, thoughts of her remained rooted in my mind long after she'd gone.

Insomnia

You were a beautiful dream.
And me?
I'm wide awake, lying here in bed with the sun
breaking through the curtains, desperately trying to
fall back asleep and find myself back in your arms.

Tinkerer

Walk into my machinarium, and show me your
broken heart.
I will open my chest to salvage the parts that were
left behind long ago.
I promise to do my best to fix yours.

She walked into his little shop, dragging a finger across a dust settled surface, leaving a dirt free trail. Sun rays shot through the few clean portions of windows, providing enough light to see the man that sat in the corner, tinkering away. "We're closed" he exclaimed, never lifting his head from his desk. The sign on the front door had not shown "open" for a long time, but it was not enough to deter the patron as she approached, holding out an item in her hands to the man's back, as if to present it to him.

She hesitated, "it's broken."

When there was no response, the woman stepped over to the side of the work bench and place the item on the table. It wasn't for a few minutes until the patron moved, unsure if the man even looked up from his tinkering to see what she had placed down. But before she could take the item back, the man reached over to a small chest in the corner of his table, dug his hand through a few knick-knacks and pulled out what looked like an old clock. It didn't make a sound, however. He moved quickly to salvage some parts from it, simultaneously taking the curio left by the woman who now sat in wait on a stool by the door. A few twists and turns and a loud ticking sound began resonating the tiny space from the tiny piece.

"Fixed."

Cotton Candy Wishes

I had always dreamt of clouds.
And when the moment came that I could reach out
and touch one, I found out there was nothing to
hold onto.

Time Capsule

We promised to come back, after all these years, no matter how far apart we were from each other. But as I stand here with a shovel in my hand, I can't help but realize I'm here alone. Maybe some things aren't worth digging up. Maybe some memories are just better left buried in the past.

Ember

"This is for the best," you said to me.

"This is for the best," you said as you watched me walk on burning coals mixed with shards of glass.

"This is for the best," you said trying to speed up the healing process after you cut into me, by burning into me the fact that you no longer loved me.

"This is for the best," you said even after I told you, you had a piece of my heart. You still chose to cut yourself out of the relationship and cauterize the wounds you knew you would be leaving.

"This is for the best," you said to me. But really, this was what you were telling yourself.

<u>Skip</u>

I have a playlist of songs that tell the story of us, that remind me of you. A playlist of songs that were my favorite at one point, that was overplayed over the course of a summer. It's a playlist of songs that I don't listen to anymore but I don't have the heart to delete. It's a playlist that doesn't feel like it anymore but entitled 'home'.

If A Tree Falls

I need to ask a question.
If a tree falls in the forest, and nobody is around to hear it, does it make a sound?
The answer isn't important, but I just wondered if you cared enough to give it a second thought.

Here's another question, but I'll need the answer to this one.
If my heart breaks, and you weren't there to hear it, did our relationship really happen? Did our love really exist?

I mean, it had to have happened. Because something has to grow in order for it all to collapse. You would know, you were the one that yelled "timber" as you watched us fall apart. But you left before I could hit the ground. The worst part was, you were the one that carried the axe into the forest that night.

So tell me, if a heart breaks, and no one is there to hear it, did you ever really love me?

IV.   The Part Where You Should Invest In
        A Parachute (And Fall In Love Again)

Pixie Dust

Thank you for having the courage to believe in me
when no one else would. Thank you for allowing me
to chase my dreams when everyone else says I need
to grow up. Thank you for keeping me grounded
because I know I can't live in the clouds all day.
Thank you for giving me the direction I need,
otherwise I'd still be out here chasing shadows. It
wasn't just dust for you, there was magic about it.
You chose to fly with me and I am grateful you did.
Thank you for finding this lost boy.
Thank you for being the Wendy to my Peter Pan.

Sign Language

Because I'll need to learn how to communicate with you whenever you leave me speechless.

Ice Cream

You will always be one of my favorite memories. I
hear your voice like the sound of an ice cream truck.
I run out and chase after you with a pocket full of
love, and hold my hand out, hoping it was enough
for you.

Taste Of Summer

She is the ice cold glass of water on a hot day. As if a sweltering heat makes me want her, need her, crave her. The moment I feel her on my lips will be blissful anticipation leading into refreshing relief.

Kaleidoscope

She is the full spectrum of emotions, I see something
new every time I turn to her. She is excitement as it
collides with joy, turning into hope, then changes to
wonder. She has me wondering what life was ever
like before her. She has me believing in the
unimaginable, and constantly aiming for the
impossible. She is my past, transforming into the
present, and shaping our future. She is the girl of my
dreams that exists in reality. She is the reflection of
the best parts of me. She is a kaleidoscope of
everything I've ever loved. I will never get tired of
looking at her.

<u>Intravenous</u>

I'll wake up each morning and feel the thoughts of you dripping life into my veins.

Gift Wrapped

The *past* is something I'll learn from.
The *future* is something I'm excited for.
But every second, every moment I get to spend with
you is the *present* I never want to take for granted.

Clocks

I swear, I can time travel with you next to me.

When I look into your eyes, my time ceases to exist. The next two hours pass in two seconds. When I look into your eyes, I can see my future. I see the eyes I want to stare into tomorrow morning, I can see the next fifty years, I see the soul of the person I want to spend the rest of my life with.

Queen Of Hearts

1.9%
1 in 52 to be exact.

Those are the chances of pulling the card that you've
been looking for. She smiled, then looked at me and
asked,
"Is this your card?"

It's called magic for a reason.

<u>William's Rocket</u>

But somehow, our stars found a way to cross paths.
A collision course that defied the heavens
themselves. Our paths were forever altered, pulled
into each other's gravity.

Ubiquitous

There's a time and a place for everything.

Except her.

I think about her everywhere, all the time.

Tourist Attraction

The dimples from her smile mapped the landmarks on her face that I loved to visit. Her kisses were the destinations my lips always arrived at. I never intended to stay, but she is where I call home.

Exhibit

There's a museum in your mind I'd like to explore, with galleries of the portraits you've painted. Each with their own storied past. Let me walk through these corridors of your history. I'll share my thoughts if you like, but yours are the ones that I came to hear. You, after all, are the original artist that's curated these walls.

<u>Cursive</u>

"Write it down, or else you'll forget it."

My pen speaks your name too often,
you are the only calligraphy it cares for.

Angel Wings

I've stumbled across feathers floating around the city, knowing angels walk among us, and their wings flutter nearby.

"Excuse me, but your halo is showing."

'Tis The Season

The memories of you are as unique as snowflakes, as they fall from above and land with soft kisses. The thoughts of you will keep me warm, as your name lingers in cold air whispers. May I decorate your face with the smiles that I've placed in boxes and tucked away? I've just been saving them for something special. I've gift wrapped our conversations, and wait patiently, knowing one day I'll open them up with childlike excitement. Make me believe in magic again.

Palpitations

You rest your head on my chest and begin to worry. I'll reassure you I'm okay.

"My heart's been skipping beats ever since I first heard your voice."

Coded

She turned those downs to ups ever since she flipped my world upside down. I'm here standing on ceilings, bouncing off walls, head over heels for her. She was right, but never left me, and was always the direction I was headed towards. Before 'her' was forgettable. After 'her' is unimaginable. It all really starts with her, and never ends. Life becomes a game of infinite possibility. She has me floating on air and falling for her all at the same time. She likes playing games with physics, but never with my heart.

Extended Play

I said "hello", she said "hi"
I said "you've got a pretty smile"
She said "you've got a one track mind"

But I wasn't trying to be her one hit wonder.
I had that LP feel, that vinyl feel, that classic feel.
I wanted to show her that album quality love, let her
listen to that chart topping love, go platinum with
that record breaking love.
I had this heart stopping type love, this soul soothing
type love.

I didn't have just this single track, but a jukebox on
my mind ready to play the entire collection for her
type love.

The Climb

When your head grows weary from the burden of the weight in your mind, do not hesitate to rest it on my shoulders. These peaks will provide solace to your traveled heart. Let me unburden your soul, so that you may continue along your journey in the morning.

Tempest

I will love you like a flash flood, showering you with kisses until your umbrella can no longer hold itself together.

Weak

Knees buckle.
Hands tremble.
Heart stops.

Strawberry Kisses

The pieces you've left can no longer satisfy my palate, for the sweetness in your lips leaves an aftertaste that has me craving all of you.

Eye Contact

I've been window shopping for a soul to love. I saw yours and couldn't pull away. I knew exactly what I had been looking for.

Pancakes

I'll make you breakfast in the morning.

But tonight, let me taste your stories, fill my cup with conversation, and I'll savor the flavor of your name as it lingers on tip of my tongue.

<u>Music</u>

Strum my heartstrings with delicate fingers. Play to my soul. I'm falling in love with you, with each note you speak. I will never grow tired of you, you always put me in the right mood. You are the loveliest of love songs.

<u>Magnetic</u>

She was worried I would be repulsed by her, but
how could I be. Her love is a magnet that pulls me
in, and alters logic and reason for her positivity only
attracts more positivity.

Treasure Chest

No jewels.

No gold pieces.

No silver coins.

Just a single heart that beats for you.

<u>Ellipsis</u>

We were two different people, a walking, breathing, loving juxtaposition. For a second, let us omit our past and focus on the most important part of our relationship.

… I loved you.

Eye Of The Storm

She is a storm. Uncontrollable. Unpredictable. She
is furious. She is calm. She is passionate and
unstoppable. She leaves a trail of chaos in her wake.
You can try and prepare for her, but she'll surprise
you in every way. Men fear her. And at first, so did
I. But as strong as the winds blow, and as loud as
the thunder roars, she strikes with the brilliance of
lightning that replaces my fear with an excitement
and amazement. Maybe out of courage, or out of
stupidity, but I no longer hold any fear. Perhaps it's
because it's too late. I've found myself caught in the
middle, and with no way out. There's no way to
escape it. There is no safer place than right in the
middle of it, the eye of the storm. There's nowhere
I'd rather be than right here. In her eyes.

Coastal Love

Let
me be
your
lighthouse.
I promise
to guide
your
path,
to keep
you safe
and to
show you
the way
back home

If
you
ever find you've
lost your way

Work

Love takes work.

But you, you'd be my dream job. It wouldn't just be some 9-5. I'd come in early, I'd leave late, I'd put in the overtime. I'll see you on weekends and holidays. I'll put in the hours. I'll never call in sick, because you make me better. I don't have vacation days, you are my getaway. If you let me, I'll take my work home with me, I'd be more than happy to.

You aren't just my 9-5. You're my 24/7, 365.

Mint Chocolate Chip

Not everyone is going to love you, but you'll always
be my favorite.

Infallible

Love her with such an unmistakable, honest, passionate love, that she questions if she's ever actually been in love before.

!

You are the exclamation mark that punctuates my
existence!
Without you, this life is just a sentence.
And these memories just fragments.
With no emotion.
No excitement

Star Struck

She was so infatuated with cold winter nights, she'd
run down sidewalks with the Christmas lights above
her head, because she said they looked like stars and
she felt like she was traveling through space.
I wasn't going to be the one to correct her and tell
her, her stars were just street lamps. Instead, I ran
alongside her, trying to keep her safe while she made
wishes on galaxies not so far away.

<u>Backpackers</u>

I'll carry the weight that you bring with you. I'll do what I can to lighten your load. But have patience with me, because I have baggage of my own.

Post Credits

Stay with me, just a little longer.
We'll wait here hoping there's more to come.
Because sometimes, it's not over until the last scene
after the credits roll. We'll either see something that
keeps us wanting more, or just find ourselves sitting
in the dark.

Rorschach

"What do you see here?, "he asked me.

Her.
I see her in places she has no business being.
Interpreting inkblots with no rhyme or reason, these images only hold the meaning she gave me. Her shadows stain my life with the remnants of our memories.
There is no right or wrong answer.
Just her.

<u>Fire Escape</u>

We ran down the stairwell to get away from it all, but who knew this would be where we'd end up, kissing in a fire escape, reigniting a relationship that had burst into flames.

Phantom Heart

You found a way to love me when I no longer had
the heart to give you. It's been gone for a while
now. Gone along with any love that I can remember
feeling. Years after losing her, like the ghost of
cardiac unrest haunting a hollow chest, it is pain that
is left behind, with faint cries left to echo through
empty corridors and chambers. I will understand if
you leave, but I will do my best to love you with this
phantom heart.

V.   Or A Toolbox (And Fall Apart Again)

Momentum

Falling in love is like playing on the swings.
It takes a lot of effort to start off, but once you get
to the top, it gets easier. Sometimes all you see is the
sky and can almost touch the clouds, and other
times, you're looking down and hoping not to fall.
You knew what you were doing, and started out fast,
while I struggled. Eventually, we both got the hang
of it. But at some point, you weren't having fun
anymore. I asked you to stay, but you jumped off
instead. I was too scared to jump. I just didn't want
to stop, but you left, and it wasn't the same. The
momentum stopped. Eventually, I'll get to the point
where I can just walk off too, without getting hurt.
But for now, I'm sitting on this swing hoping to get
to the top again.

<u>Poison</u>

She will destroy you and you won't know it until it's too late. You'll kiss her without knowing the venom that coats her lips.

The Heist

I was met with signs that read, "No Trespassing."

So you gave me the blueprints.
But you forgot to mention the electric fences that left me with burn marks, or the barbed wire that left me with these scars. When I reached your heart, I still had to pick the locks to steal your love. But I had it. I thought I did. And that's when you went quiet and I was just left with radio silence. You made your great escape and I can't help but think I've come away with nothing but a forgery.

Capture Effect

I'll still hear your voice in the background, as if my brain is switching between radio stations only to hear your song on every frequency. Everything else just sounds like static.

Autumn Leaves

I fell for you like countless leaves do, but you kicked me aside. You said I wasn't the same person you fell in love with but you're the one whose colors changed. Now my branches are left bare, holding onto what leaves remain that still carry memories of summer.

Desperado

The sun beats down from the highest point in the sky. There's a bounty on my head but a girl on my mind. We were outlaws in love, breaking the rules of the game. Partners in crime caught up in this new frontier. Who knew this runaway train would eventually catch up to us. When it comes down to renegades, someone will eventually get hurt. Now we're left trying to see eye to eye, in a standoff at high noon. My hands shake with terrified anticipation, because I know I can't pull the trigger. There will be no riding off into the sunset today. Just the sunset.

Sand

Every time we fought, our relationship sunk deeper
into trouble. And yet, the tighter I held on, the
faster you slipped away as bits of you fell through my
fingers, running out the seconds on our glass timer.
It was only after our time had run out that I
considered turning back the clock, but I knew if I
did, we would eventually end up back here again.

<u>Candy Man Confections</u>

She grew tired of his sugarcoated lies, and could taste the poison behind his artificial sweetness. Deceits, carefully and individually wrapped in empty promises, she could stomach no more.

"But, what would one more piece hurt?"

Shards

We were a broken relationship, a pair of shattered glass hearts. Pieces of you cut deep, leaving scars with fragments of you still in me, long after you've left. I held out my hands as they dripped with the memories of us. Bandages couldn't stop the bleeding, as you slipped out of my life.

"It's too late, she's gone."

Sweater Weather

She loved your oversized sweaters.
They felt like one long hug that kept her warm. That
kept her safe. That took care of her and protected
her. After you said she could keep it, it seemed to
lose its magic. She didn't feel quite as warm. She
saw the holes that let the cold in, she saw the threads
that unraveled themselves. She didn't feel safe, or
protected. Now, she just felt trapped, wearing a
wool straight jacket.
She outgrew you and your weathered sweater.

Overdose

Nostalgia is a drug I've taken too often. Drunk off one too many memories, I've woken up with terrible hangovers of you the next morning. I'm addicted to revisiting my past when I should just let it go, leave it be. Instead, there's always that craving, that desire to go back. That promise to myself that this would be the last time.

Fishbowl

I'm tired of us swimming the same circles, around familiar castles. There has to be more to life outside these glass walls. But your kisses taste like amnesia, making me forget whatever it was that we were fighting about.

"Oh, look, a castle!"

Scribble

My pen quivers, as any mark on this blank page
becomes permanent, bound forever with what is left,
no matter what mistakes are made. I cannot erase
you, and scratching you out will only leave greater
scars. I thought this had to be flawless, but fear
cannot dictate these unwritten words. So I'll make
my mistakes, because the editing process is long and
ongoing. No story is born perfect.

House Of Cards

I was the king and she was my queen. But we never
noticed our relationship was built like a house of
cards with not-so-steady hands. And when our
castle crumbled, there was no one left standing, there
was no more fighting for the top. Only a pile of
cards to be picked up and rebuilt over again hoping
things wouldn't fall apart this time.

<u>Fractured</u>

The cracks in our relationship have grown into the size of canyons. You can't understand why now I'm hesitant to build bridges for you, when you had your chances to build them before, to jump across when the distance wasn't so wide, or to simply stand next to me before our world eroded.

<u>Fertilizer</u>

A relationship is the flower that you thought was beautiful, and decided to pick. But it's not enough to just pick the flower, you must give it a home, water it, allow the sun to shine on it. You must give it the nourishment it needs. Give it somewhere safe to settle roots. Because once those petals dry and fall, there is no saving it.

Potpourri is still the result of something that has died, and break-ups don't smell as sweet.

In Memory Of Us

You're standing on the grave of a relationship that
has passed, of loves that have died, where hearts
have been buried, and "forevers" have expired. May
these souls that once crossed paths find their own
way home and one day find their peace.

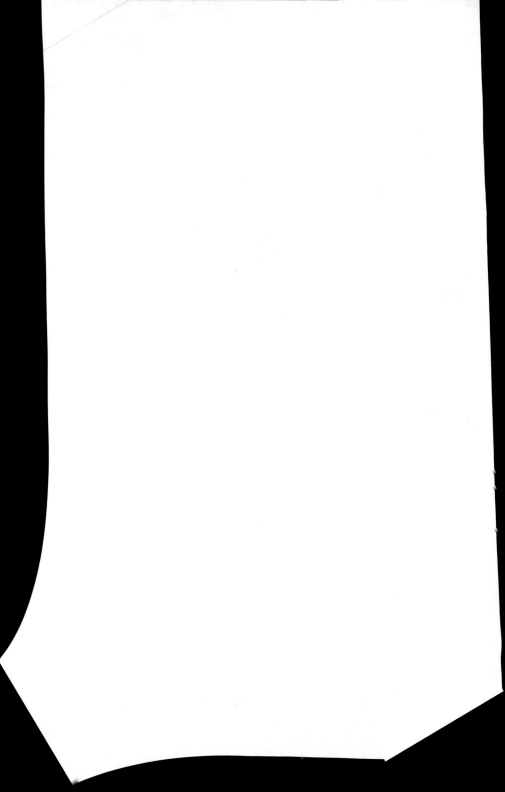

VI.   The Part Where You Invest In Yourself

Definition

def·i·ni·tion
/defə'niSH(ə)n/
1) *n.* It is okay to be the *subject* and focus on yourself
from time to time. 2) *v.* But allow yourself to be an
action predicated on things like love, hope, and virtue.
Compliment others, remembering you are part of a
bigger picture, a larger community. 3) Do not wear
any single label, allow yourself to be defined by more
than one thing. 4) Allow your life to have multiple
meanings and your name be synonymous with many
connotations.

<u>Nemesis</u>

I'm sorry I hurt you. It was never what I wanted. I understand I'll be the villain in your story, but now I wonder if I'm even the hero in mine.

Masquerade

Our smiles hide what we're afraid others might see.
They're masks that keep our demons in the dark.
We've been guests at this party for so long, we've
forgotten what it's like to not be wearing our
costumes anymore.

Giants

On the shoulders of giants, I've found to be a view like no other. A vastness of lands that stretch to the furthest reaches of our vision. On the shoulders of giants I see my past, riddled with mistakes in the form of mirages. These hallucinations of things we had thought to have perceived that did not exist. Mistakes that form oases that we had not seen but wish we did. On the shoulders of giants we see the futures, paths that we will follow, oceans we must cross. Guaranteed, we will struggle. We will fail. But failure is the growth that has created our giants. Our failures have created the rungs on the ladder of which we climb and sit atop success, as we peer at the horizon of opportunity. On the shoulders of giants, before us and presently, we stand tall and proud.

Undiagnosed Loneliness

I never needed a psychologist. I already felt like a
burden, so for a complete stranger to want to listen
to my problems always seemed absurd to me.
And paying for someone to act like they cared only
made it seem even more ridiculous.

"I never needed a doctor,
 I just wanted a friend."

Daylight Savings

Today will be the closest I'll come to time travel and all it will take is to simply change the hands of the clock. If only these hands could change my past so easily. If I could just get a few thousand days like this, maybe I can fix some of the mistakes I've made.

<u>Fear</u>

This is where the shadows refuse to disappear, but grow to the size of towering giants. This is where pain roots itself in, and grows like weeds. This is where hope fades slowly beneath a fog of looming despair. It's in the darkest corners of my mind where I refuse to be consumed by these shadows. This is where I'll use the nightmare fuel to set my soul on fire, and find my way out back into the light.

Yellow Bricks & Scared Crows

I never said I wasn't scared. I'm terrified. Every day, I wake up, I'm scared. Before I go to sleep, I lie in bed for hours because I'm afraid. But the world is filled with scary things. You just do your best to be brave. And when you're not brave enough, I'll be here to remind you that even lions forget about their courage sometimes.

Window Pains

The eyes are the windows to the soul, and looking into mine, you'll see why I've always tried to hide behind curtains. I was afraid that you'd see through me, every streak and scratch. And no matter how clear the view appears, these pains can never truly be wiped clean of the dirt from my past. No matter how well you think you can see me, there will always be a part of me that will feel invisible.

Piggybank

Great change doesn't happen all at once, it happens a little bit each day. It takes time and patience to accumulate, but one day, you'll have enough change to buy freedom.

Undefined

They say you are an average of the people that surround you. So what does that mean if I see no one around? You cannot divide by zero.

<u>Seadogs</u>

Do not listen to the captain that tells you to not
make waves.
Every boat, no matter the size or speed, will make
waves in its journey. Even dead bodies floating in
the water make ripples. But you have yet to
succumb to Davy Jones's locker, so there are no
excuses here. You will tell your stories of
exploration, bravery, survival, and let them be carried
on the sails of your ships, with your flags flying
proudly atop your vessel.
Do not apologize for the waves you make, no sea
legends have ever come from still waters.

Snow Prints

Your boots used to make boat sized holes in the snow. You always walked ahead, and I hopped along behind you, bouncing from one hole to the other. But the longer we walked in the storm, the more the snow filled in those boot prints. At some point, they just disappeared, and you were gone in the whiteout. You were no longer there to guide me, there were no more footsteps to follow, and from here on out, I had to make my own tracks.

<u>Keyholes</u>

You saw a shut door so you looked through the
keyhole, always wondering what was on the other
side but never bothered to turn the knob and realize
it was unlocked all along.

<u>Harry Houdini</u>

You had a tendency to come and go, and always when I least expected it.

"Greatest Escape Artist", "Renowned Illusionist", "The Premier Performer". Call yourself whatever you'd like but don't say you were here for me. I grew tired of watching the same disappearing act again and again. The show has gone on for too long, and I refuse to be your audience any longer.

No more tricks.

The magic is gone.

The curtains have closed.

The Gallery

I was a lone patron left to wander these museum halls, unsure if, in actuality, I was the one wearing the frame, as a single piece left to be judged beneath hushed tones. I stared at eyes that stared right back, as conversations played out between myself and these paintings. I was trying to figure out their story while looking for mine. I asked questions that I wanted to know the answers to, hearing echoed wisdom, spoken through whispers in my head. I conveyed aspirations that I had failed to live up to, to the kindness of canvass silence. In some of the paintings, I'd divulge my darkest secrets, so I could feel I wasn't the only one that carried my burdens. It was nice to have someone to listen to, even if they were born of acrylic.

Tetris

Some days I feel like the writer's blocks fall from the
sky, building up faster than I can take them down.
And I'm just hoping to stumble upon the right piece
to finally clear this wall. But as soon as I do, the
blocks start coming again.

Some of the hardest days are ones where I run out of
words. Some of the darkest fears are of running out
of stories. And my words aren't good enough, and
they stop holding meaning. Some days, I question if
these words are even worth reading.

Some days, I don't feel like playing anymore,
I don't feel like writing anymore.
Some days, the only words I see on my screen are
"Game Over".

Golden Eggs

"Don't cry over spilled milk."
Not every glass holds the same weight. It's easier to
see the glass half full if the farmer has a full herd of
cattle, but some of us don't own a herd. Some of us
have just the one cow. The one cow that we've sold
to someone who promised us magic. And while
others were given beanstalks to climb, some were
just given beans. We aren't all as lucky as Jack.
Sometimes, if someone spills milk, let them cry, tell
them it's okay, and just remind them you're there to
help clean it up.

Artifacts

This is unexplored territory. I haven't stepped foot in these ruins for a long time. It's easy to find the love that I write about over and over again, but these paths of self-discovery and reflection have not been walked through in years. I've allowed the rubble to bury my emotions so deep making it difficult for anyone who cared enough to try to dig up. The walls of my mind have been engraved with hieroglyphs; without any translation, and written so long ago, it's as if they were only made to be forgotten. Raid these ancients if you'd like. You'll run your fingers over these carvings, hoping to find ways to understand, but I'll warn you, there may not be much left to uncover here. You may not find anything but tombs.

<u>Blueprint</u>

Use today to build the future with the foundation of the past.

Celestial Envy

City lights will line city skies trying their best to imitate the stars above. For poems of love and romance are written of these celestial beings that have been said to guide lost souls. But what we do not see is how those starry skies sparkle green with envy of city lights. For while everyone wishes on stars, the people who stay up at night are not merely wishing for their dreams to come true, they are willing their dreams true. They chase those wishes instead of watching them shoot by. These lights are ignited from sore hands, stressed minds, and overworked souls. They burn their lights bright, and let their lives shine to remind the universe of their existence. They will not disappear behind grey clouds, or burn out like red giants. City lights will shine during the darkest nights, tell stories of unrelenting desire, and refuse to be lost in the darkness.

Flicker

Do not hesitate to let someone know if they've impacted your life for the better. We are all candles that flicker from time to time, struggling to stay lit in the darkness. Encourage others to reignite their flames instead of extinguishing them.

Raindrop

What is a raindrop to the cloud? She felt as if she held no power, told she was small, and would be lost in the flood. And with the weight of all that negativity around her, she fell.

But in falling, she will rise. And bring the rest of the storm with her. She has no idea of the lightning that runs through her veins or the thunder in her voice.

Sleepless

3 a.m. is reserved for the sleepless dreamers, for
some patrons may stumble in, but the regulars are
the ones who've claimed seats here.

3 a. m. is reserved for the poets whose pens refuse to
sleep and madmen whose minds remain just as
restless.

3 a.m. is when the two become indistinguishable, and
when their lights simultaneously fade and glow.

3 a.m. is for the fairytales that refuse to lose magic at
midnight. It's a time where mistakes are made,
details are lost, and stories are told.

3 a.m. is reserved for us.

The Icarus Effect

The sky is an infinite escape we only dream to explore. To swim in the blue oceans above, and dance through clouds. I can give you the stars but I must be able to reach them first. It will take time to get off the ground, for flight is something that was never gifted to us. If you don't believe in my ability to fly, that is fine. But do not cut my wings off.

Do not mourn those whose wings catch fire. We were never meant to fly so close to the sun, asked only to adorn it from a distance. But celebrate the magnificence of their fulfilled lives, for only those willing to fall, are the ones that can say they've touched greatness.

<u>Pulse</u>

It was hard to see the scars that ran across her forearms, because I knew she always wore her heart on her sleeve. But those scars paint the picture of depression and pain, ones that she's struggled with, but more importantly, that she persevered through. And no matter how cut up or broken her heart was, it is still beating and ready to love with open arms, with reckless vulnerability, with courage and trust. Remember that when she lets you hold her in your arms, you hold her heart in your hands too.

Lois Lane

Don't idolize Lois Lane, or choose to be her.
She is not worthy of the hope in your heart or the
symbol on your chest.

Because Clark Kent is still Superman without his
cape. And Lois Lane refuses to see the hero, until
everyone else deems him to be super. Don't tell me
those bright red and blue tights can't be seen
through that white shirt. Because glasses don't
suddenly make you invisible. And it shouldn't take
jumping over the edges of buildings to be seen.
Don't make me fight constantly for your attention,
I've got enough villains to fight. Don't be the girl
hiding behind me, or waiting for me to save her.
Stand next to me, fight beside me, and we'll watch
the world from above the clouds.

Be my Wonder Woman, and I promise to be your
Man of Steel.

Rest

I'm exhausted.
Can we just stop and rest, just for a little while?

I promise, tomorrow, we'll follow more dreams and
clouds. We'll pursue every sunrise and sunset if that
means we find happiness. But right now, I'm tired.
Tired of running from my demons. My legs can no
longer carry me, and I can feel the pain catching up.
I just don't have the energy to keep going. Please, let
me close my eyes, let me rest here.

Tonight, we can watch the stars go by.
Maybe tomorrow, we'll chase them again.

<u>Bully</u>

They built your walls.

                                        Demolish them.

<u>Aftermath</u>

The sky is empty from where I once stood. I felt the impending collapse as tremors took their toll on the stability of my foundation, until I no longer had the support to hold myself up. I tried to catch the debris of my life with the pages of my notebook. Maybe I can build something out of the rubble of words left from everything that has fallen apart.

Terminal Thoughts

Do you ever find yourself people-watching at airports? Wondering where people are going, who they're leaving, or who they're coming home to? Who are they running from or what it is they're chasing? Or wonder what kind of baggage fits in a suitcase?

No? Yeah, me neither.

Tattoo

Because you have scars that were given to you, ones you never asked for, and ones that people have judged you by. But these ones are the ones you've chosen to give yourself as reminders that as skin breaks, stories break through and that beauty and meaning can, without a doubt, come from pain. These scars are not simply graffiti left by careless passers-by, but the writings you've left on your own walls that now paint the mural that is you.

Kings

I sat in my grandfather's office, a small box lay on the desk with a note addressed, "Practice."

I opened it, and inside found a marble chess piece. I held the King in my hand, and remembered the lessons taught.

Your first move is key.

Every decision is important.

Protect your queen, for she is strong and will protect you.

Plan for the future.

You will make mistakes, learn from them.

Loss is inevitable and sacrifice is crucial.

Every game ends, but that doesn't mean you stop playing.

There was a reason he taught me this game.

Ripped Jeans

After years of falling on my hands, and scraping my skin, after coming home countless times with bloody palms rubbed dry with dirt and grass, I'd get constant reminders from my mother telling me to take care of myself and the jeans that I had a habit of tearing. I never really learned my lesson to not rip my jeans, but I also never really expected these ripped jeans to be as popular as they are. I didn't expect them to be so edgy or desirable, and turn into the next trend. I didn't expect ripped jeans to be sold everywhere, or be worn by everyone, but I guess it's easier to buy them instead of having to go through the pain of falling again. As a kid tripping over myself on the playground, I never expected to use ripped jeans as a metaphor for broken hearts. I guess everyone has a pair of ripped jeans in their closet.

Quicksand

You're caught up in a habit of watching sand fall
through the cracks. But it isn't sand that slips
through the crevices, it's the ashes of cremated
dreams that rain down through your glass timer.
These dreams die daily; and when it's over, you
simply turn the dial and let yourself disappear again.
Your arms and legs move instinctively, struggling to
stay afloat, but you're swimming
in sand, and drowning in a
desert of routine
exhaustion.

Stop.

Relax.

Breathe.

Take
your time
to enjoy what is important,
and maybe you'll find yourself building castles on a
beach instead of sinking in quicksand.

These Blank Pages

I am an open book, but my pages are empty. My words were written with the whisper of a pen pressed too lightly on the page to leave any marks. I have an unsharpened confidence, my pencil couldn't even speak if you asked me to. No one would want to read my story anyway. So here I am, spilling ink on these blank pages hoping some of it makes sense.

<u>Sharp</u>

Words are just words.

Until they become lies. And those lies turn to knives. Sharpened by the tongue. And pushed in your back.

Sticks and stones break your bones, but words cut deeper than we were raised to believe.

Snake Eyes

I understand there is no honor amongst thieves, that
I am gambling with my life when I entrust it with
you. You've stacked the deck but I see your
bleeding hands. I see the lies you tell, the tricks that
you pull. You throw loaded dice and when it's all
said and done, I'll stare right through your snake
eyes.

Denial

When a girl
or boy meet someone they
trust and love,
they don't always
see the signs,
or the danger.

"He's just that way"
"She didn't mean it"
"It was my fault"
"It's not a problem"

It's hard to see, but once you do,
things are never the same again.

<u>Simba's Pride</u>

I hear stories of how you've become king. You boast of how you've climbed to the top, but keep silent of those you've let down in order to hold onto your pride rock. The problem is, I hear your lies loud and clear, like the laugh of hyenas. You once called me brother, but then sunk your claws into my skin, leaving scars on my back that resemble the Scar in your eyes. But no matter how many times you let me fall, this lion will always rise.

Catacombs

My notebook is a graveyard of stories, poems and thoughts. Many of which have been long buried away. My pen has not only carved their tombstones, but has dug the graves of these lost ideas, forgotten fragments and unfinished works.

But as I turn back the pages to pay my respects, I cannot help but reinvigorate the mad scientist inside, my Jekyll gives way to my Hyde. I will reanimate these corpses, and breathe these words back to life.

VII. The Part Of Your Future That Is
      Running Late

E.T.A.

You must have missed your flight, I was told you'd be here by now but you're running late. Don't worry, I'll still be here when you arrive, with a bouquet of flowers in my hand and your name written on my smile.

<u>Odyssey</u>

I'm not sure where the destination is but I hope my journey leads us to cross paths. Until then, I will paint hearts on these moisture ridden windows with my fingers, in hopes that they find you before fading away. I'll watch as these raindrops hold the lights from the street lamps, and make wishes as they mimic shooting stars passing by.

<u>Origami Love</u>

I'll write you love notes inside origami cranes, so my words have the wings to reach you wherever you may be.

Be gentle as you unfold my paper heart.

Andromeda

She pulls on my heart strings until they become tightropes which she dances across because tiptoeing has never been her style. She was never afraid of falling as she dances above the heavens. Angels are jealous of her, because she has no wings and yet she finds ways to fly. She turns cherubims into cherry blossoms, relegating them to wall flowers as she takes center stage in the clouds. She will choreograph constellations with each and every step she takes.

<u>Velocity</u>

Love and velocity have the same equation.

Distance over time plus direction.

The distance is not measured in how far you are away from me. I will love you no matter the distance between us, no matter how far you are. The distance that matters is in how far we've come. That distance will always be greater than the waters, mountains and roads that may separate us.

Time. Do not examine what is measured in seconds, minutes, hours, but in holidays with your family, lazy nights indoors or nights out on the town. The time divided between the two of us, between days that I can hardly wait to see you. The times that we've struggled, cried and laughed. It is that time we've spent with each other that counts. I will love you forever and always, I don't fear your past and can only greet our future with a smile. Time can never be zero. I will always value our time.

Lastly, direction is important, otherwise, the equation is incomplete. The direction our love takes is what makes this velocity and not just speed. I don't care which direction we go, which road we take, as long as I'm right there by your side. I'm traveling in the direction that leads to, and keeps me with you.

<u>Pull</u>

Love   will
  bring   us
    closer   together
        until   there
          is   only
        you&me

<u>True Fiction</u>

I want our story to be so unbelievable, so unreal, people will question if it really happened.

Paper Boats

"You are beautiful"

"You are important"

"You matter"

"You make me happy"

"I miss you"

"I love you"

These words, these phrases, are secrets my lips tell your ears. They repeat them daily, speak them proudly, and don't care who knows them. They are not secrets because they are kept from others, but they are secrets. For these words are meant for you, and only you. I trust you with these words, they are yours to keep.

They are notes hidden daily in your subconscious. So whenever you need to hear these words, they will be somewhere you know where to find them.

They are folded pieces of paper in class that I will always get caught passing to you. Because there is no better time to tell you than now, there is no better time to tell you than forever, there is no better time to tell you than always. And when they ask me to read it out loud, I'll yell it at the top of my lungs, standing on my desk.

Oh captain, my captain, I am in love with you. Carry me along your waves, let me drown in your smile, I am ready to sink into your arms, drown in your depths, I will go down with this ship. I surrender to you.

Blessed

The moment I knew I loved you was the moment I realized you were everything I prayed for.

Not because I prayed for you specifically, but because I asked God for patience, understanding, wisdom, and strength…

And He sent me you.

Savant

She said I did too much, that it wasn't needed, and that simply loving her was enough. But I couldn't help it. I enjoyed every second I had to study her and each detail of her being. She is fascinating to say the least, and I have never found it difficult to memorize the way that she moves, the intricacies of her smile, or the way she says what she says. There is still too much about her to not want to delve deeper. But there isn't enough time on this earth to not want to dedicate my life to learning everything there is to know about her. If loving her dictates me a scholar, then she will be my Nobel Prize.

Lift Off

Waiting for you in the early morning, we snuck out at dusk, stealing the keys to the rocket ship. My fingers outline the constellations of your goosebumps as we navigate through this highway of burning comets. We arrive to the launch site, where the stars are brighter than the city lights, and I've begun the countdown.

T minus 10 seconds, my heart is racing
9, your eyes are watching the sky
8, the sun will rise
7, but I can't take my eyes off you
6, I'd like to kiss you
5, so I'll take your hand
4, and pull you close
3, and you're eyes will shift
2, and see me
1…

This is what it must feel like for astronauts traveling through space. And no matter the journey, you will always be the destination.

Come Find Me

For some reason, these three words are ingrained in me, echoing off the walls of every piece that's manifested from these thoughts, they whisper to me every time I write anew. They are reminders of promises I don't remember making, promises that I hold guilt over, for I can't help but feel I've let someone down, that I let you down. Because I've failed to keep true to the words of your unrelenting search. So until the day comes that I've found you, I have no answers. Only three words of an unfinished poem.

Long Exposure

In these darkrooms, I will develop my favorite memories of you. They are candid because you were always too camera shy to let me snap anything more than the mental images of the girl I loved. Framed perfectly, and always in focus, you were the only subject that ever mattered. A thousand words would never do you justice, so I will turn our love story into a collection of moments, that will fill the thousands of pages of our photo albums.

Queen Of Hearts II

Pick a poem, any love poem.
Now memorize it.
And put it back.

When I read it out loud, you'll know it was yours.
But it's not hard to figure out the trick to my magic,
because I'm playing with a rigged deck.
You see, every poem has a piece of my heart in it.
Every love poem was written for you.

Heartaches And Hangovers

Head spinning, heart racing, I'm drunk. Drunk on your words. Because your voice is intoxicating, and I can't help but write under your influence. I've become the sloppy poet, spilling words that I've never had the courage to tell you. I can still taste your name on my lips as I stumble across these written lines. Tomorrow morning will bring the inevitable hangover, and you, the only cure I need.

The Process

Take your time, be meticulous, see the details.
Because it is in taking the time that we know this is a
passion. If we were to rush through our work, we
simply want to get it over with and move on. But
those that can slow down, those that truly obsess
over a task, have the love for the process, the desire
to chase perfection. And that's how I'll love you. I'll
love you slowly. I'll take my time. I'll be meticulous.
I'll search for every detail, never in a rush and never
wanting to move on. I love the process of loving
you. I will chase your perfection.

R.E.M.

You are the most vivid and memorable of dreams.

And each time, I will fall deeper into you.

Small Leaps & Giant Steps

I will love you to the moon and back. But that won't be enough for me so I will refuel my rocket to return to your space again, and count down the days until I can live in your stars and travel galaxies with you. I will love you beyond infinity.

Terraforming

You are not the same girl I fell in love with, and that's okay. The earth itself is continuously changing, plates shifting, new lands forming and being discovered. There is not enough time to reread the past that fills your history book for you are constantly writing it, and I will be left behind if I am too focused on who you were. The world has changed, and formed mountains and shaped oceans. And you learned to scale those peaks and cross those waters. You aren't the same girl I fell in love with. You're the woman I wake up to each morning, giving me new experiences, and more reasons to love you.

<u>Ink</u>

You are the ink in my pen, the one that keeps me writing. Without you, there are no words. Without you, there are just scratches on an empty page. Without you, my story would have ended a long time ago.

Brimstone Princess

This is a letter I will read to you one day. Every time you go to bed, as if these words were folded at the beginning of your bedtime stories, so that they stay with you, with each "goodnight".

Dear princess, be careful of the knight in shining armor that's come to save you, for shiny armor is suspicious. What wars have been fought to reach you, what lands traversed to find you, what struggles endured, what terrors conquered, if the armor your knight wore were still to be shining?

Dear princess, they say dragons hold you captive. I will tell you they are false, for dragons do not hold you captive, nor are they to be slain, but unleashed and set free. You were born with wings to fly, and a voice that breathes fire, so use them.

Dear princess, stop waiting. Don't wait for the story to be read to you. There is too much in this world to see, to simply wait in old towers. Go and write your own adventures and one day I'll ask you to read me your story.

Dear daughter, if you do not wish to be the princess in a castle, but instead, wish to find her, then I will give you your sword and shield. And if you want to be the dragon that stories have told use to fear, then go and set the world ablaze.

A Classic & Best-Seller

Nothing beats a classic. The feel of the spine, the smell of her pages, the memories of childhood stories, the sense of hope, excitement, and wonder that comes with new adventure. I want it all.

I want to look at your eyes and know that's what draws me in. Like judging a book by its cover, there's a lot hiding behind them. And when you open up, I want you to tell me a story.
I want to start off slow, because well, there's no rush here, I'll just hang on to your every word. But I'll pick them apart and pick up the pace, because I can't stop thinking about you. I want to know what happens next. I want the surprise of a plot twist, but paired with a cliché happy ending. Because I want to know that we'll be alright, but not know how we get there. I want you to get better the longer I know you, there's new experiences in the details, just remind me to look for them. I want to come back to you when I need inspiration, because you say exactly what I need to hear.

I want to run my fingers across your skin, and feel your goosebumps like I'm reading braille. I want to pick you up, and take you to bed with me. I want to read in between your lines, and read you under the covers. I want to be able to finish your sentences because I know you by heart. I want to know your story and never forget it. One page at the beginning is not enough, I want to dedicate my life story to you.

I want you to be my favorite book.

<u>Last</u>

To the girl that I'll fall in love with next, you're it.
You're the one.
You're the last person I want to fall in love with.
Because I don't think my heart has anything left to
lose. We're hanging on by a thread here, and I don't
know if I can handle being torn apart again.
To the girl that I'll fall in love with next, this is it.
You are my forever.
But hey, no pressure.

On Blank Pages

Table of Contents

V. Or A Toolbox (And Fall Apart Again)

VI. The Part Where You Invest In Yourself

VII. The Part Of Your Future That Is Running Late

The Post-Credit Scene

Thank You

You are the reason my words exist.
Without you they mean nothing.

On Blank Pages

Giuliano Enciso

CPSIA information can be obtained
at www.ICGtesting.com
Printed in the USA
LVHW081047230123
737755LV00022B/335